Chalk Talk

vol. #1

BRYAN KENNEDY
C.P.C.

Illustrated by
Bryan Kennedy

PREFACE

Many artists and athletes are constantly under a spotlight, exposing their entire lives. Life off the field, stage, and court directly and profoundly affects performance on the field, stage, and court. Learning a healthy balance between the two, while daily seeking the right perspective and direction is what I hope you'll gain from these Chalk Talk coaching sessions

TABLE OF CONTENTS

1 Peter 5:2 (NIV)

[2] Be shepherds of God's flock that is under your care, watching over them—not because you must, but because you are willing, as God wants you to be; not pursuing dishonest gain, but eager to serve.

#1
Food for Thought

I could think of no better Chalk Talk to begin this book with than to borrow an old Cherokee Story I heard many years ago. Let us all constantly apply this wisdom as we prepare, practice, train and play in the ring of life.

"Two Wolves Within"

One evening an old Cherokee told his grandson about a battle that goes on inside people. He said, "My son, the battle is between two wolves inside us all."

One is "Evil"- it is anger, envy, jealousy, sorrow, regret, greed, arrogance, self-pity, guilt, resentment, inferiority, lies, false pride, superiority, and ego.

The other is "Good"- it is joy, peace, love, hope, serenity, humility, kindness, benevolence, generosity, empathy, truth, compassion and faith."

The grandson thought about this for a minute and then asked the grandfather, "Which wolf wins?"

BRYAN KENNEDY

The old Cherokee simply replied, "The one you feed".

#2

The Road You Are On

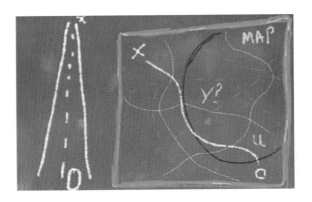

"If you stay on the road you are on,
you will end up where you are going."

I don't know if that's a quote from a famous philosopher, or maybe just a mom or dad with some common sense. Regardless, it is a great philosophy.

I heard this little quip several years ago. As simple and maybe as *duh* as it sounds, take a moment to consider its powerful truth.

Maybe you know the exact answer as to where you want to go? You may have it pinned to a map in your mind but are you getting there?

Why are you no closer to that destination than the days, weeks, months, or even years before?

Consider the moment that is *right now.*
Look at the road you are on.
Study it.

Look at what you see along this road; the people traveling with you, the things you are carrying with you, things you have packed, and maybe things you have thrown in the back seat and have forgotten all about.

Consider EVERYTHING on your road.

Is this the road that will get you to where you wish to be? There's no doubt we will all get to where the road we're on is going. You may be on the right road, and if so... keep going.

But, if we discover the road we're on isn't the road that will take us where we wish to go, we must TURN AROUND, EXIT, PULL OVER AND LOOK AT A MAP.

What map? I find the best map to be in a book like Proverbs you can find in The Bible.

#3
It's Important to Know What's Important

What's important?
I will tell you what is important... It is important that you have a list of what's important!

Being a Life coach I understand that when we are perceived to have it *all together* as athletes or creative/artistic people, everyone seems to think we couldn't possibly have thoughts, doubts, or concerns outside of our *spotlight*.

So, we need a list.

You will always, always hear me say to keep a journal! A book, spiral notebook, or just some sort of binder... a place, a collective specific binder, or book to write your thoughts down, and yes... lists.

So grab a pencil or pen and find yourself a place to write your list of what's important. Take your time and think about it. Get alone and quiet and begin to let go of all the noises and distractions around you and think about what is truly important to you. Then, find someone you can trust to discuss your list with.

#4
10-4 on 4:10

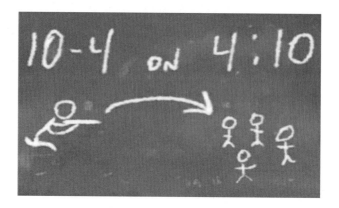

When I write songs I love bending words; stretching them, and re-shaping them. I see words as tools and missing pieces to puzzles in my writing. The right word twisted and turned a certain way can make or break a song.

Numbers? Hard to bend a number; it pretty much is what it is. Maybe that's why numbers are not as interesting to me as a songwriter, author, and playwright. But still I see them sometimes in the same way; *puzzle pieces.*

For example: *10-4* (I still love to use phrases from the CB radio days). Like, *That's a Big 10-4,* which means, *yes,* affirmative, or the more impactful, HECK YES! Changing CB channels (something you may not know), this is one of my favorite verses from the Bible:

"Each one of you should use whatever gift he has received to serve others, faithfully administering God's grace on it's various forms."- 1 Peter 4:10

When we really take hold of that verse and apply it to our lives… that's when I say, *That's a big 10-4 on 4:10.*

As athletes or artists, our gifts are obvious.
But remember, so are the ways we use (or don't use) them… because somebody, if not everybody, is watching. So let's use our gifts wisely

6

and faithfully, to serve.

And if you should see me in person, how 'bout saying, *That's a big 10-4 on 4:10.* Or say it to someone you know, or don't know... might start a good conversation.

#5
Right on…Write on

Encouraging Letters

Don't you just love receiving and reading an encouraging letter?

The Bible is full of them. The apostles wrote to entire groups of people so that they might encourage them! Example after example, we see each letter opening with encouraging remarks, assuring statements, and then each letter closing with more encouraging remarks.

Check out the beginning of the book of Philippians:

Philippians 1:3 (NIV) says, *"I thank my God every time I remember you. (4) In all my prayers for all of you, I always pray with joy (5) because of your partnership in the gospel from the first day until now, (6) being confident of this, that he who began a good work in you will carry it on to completion until the day of Christ Jesus."*

What a rich and beautiful example this is for us; simply telling someone you thank God for them. Let someone know they are in your prayers, and that you think of them with joy!

With today's technology this should be easier. Today we have email, blogs, tweets, and texts. Today it's easier than ever to fill someone's inbox with one or two sentences of assurance or encouragement.

Why don't we? Why don't you follow this world changing practice?

Write someone and open your remarks with encouraging and uplifting words. Write a group and encourage them, praise them for simple and little things you notice.

Try it. You will bless someone and be blessed.

Write On!

#6
Time for a Chalk Talk X-O-Y...U

Alright, it's time to explain X's, O's, U and Y.

Remember, when your coach gives you a chalk talk, you are always represented on the board as either an X or an O. That's in the game, but in life... in real LIFE, you are U. And U need to always keep in mind Y. Why you are here.
And if you don't know Y you are here... go find out!

So get up!

Get out!

Go!
Do something!

Do several things! Don't stop. Don't quit. Don't sit on your excuse!

Push yourself to do the things you DO NOT want to do... either for the first time, the second, third, or 100th time!

Huddle up. Call it. Break the huddle... and BOOM! See what happens... You will be amazed!

CHALK TALK

Y R U here?

#7
You are Trained for NOW

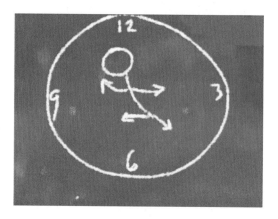

What do you think when you think about your past? Are you running from it? Are you willing to learn from it? Do you spend too much time thinking about your *awful past* or your *perfect past*? Are you are still trying to live there?

We train our whole lives for something. In fact, we train our whole lives for *right now*.

What are you going to do with right now? You have been given cuts, bumps, bruises, victories, celebrations, failures, and good and bad choices.

We hear everyday, "He's going be a great player once he has gotten more experience."

Experience isn't free and it isn't quick.

You've been in training. Take the positive and pass it on. YOU will learn from passing it on as well.

Become skilled at identifying the not so good and quickly recognize and remove yourself with grace and speed from that path.

CHALK TALK

Take the negative and pass it on as an example to others of what not to do by sharing your results. And keep training. (In other words, keep living!)

Experience = Living

You have been training for the moment called NOW.

#8
Up-Hill means...

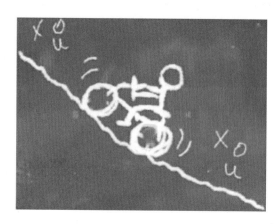

No sugar coating here.

No statistics needed.

Sometimes life is hard, so what now? Keep pedaling.
Why?
When it all seems up hill, remember two things:

      1. You're getting in better shape.

      2. And know what's coming next... downhill!

#9
I've got a Good Idea…

"A new idea is delicate. It can be killed by a sneer or a yawn; it can be stabbed to death by a quip and worried to death by a frown on the right man's brow."
— Charles Brower

I'm not familiar with Mr. Brower, but he sure hit the nail on the head. Creative people often have great, spectacular ideas that unfortunately sometimes only one person ever hears. Mr. Brower's quote recognizes and calls attention to why that is.

When a brand new idea is born, the vessel or person by which the idea is first voiced is usually very excited! They believe in it's full potential, and can clearly see the end result.

This creative person will first run to someone that they trust and *know*, and will recognize it as a great idea. But somehow no more than one person hears the idea because of their reaction.

People are mighty quick to cut a new idea down, and even quicker to be-little someone that is just *trying* to do something that maybe they don't have the skill set yet to do. But boy do they ever have a good idea.

And it all begins with an idea!

So to all you creative people; don't quit after receiving your first reaction. If you really, really believe in your new idea, keep trying! Don't let a negative first reaction you receive be the *only* reaction you receive.

I've got a good idea...the next time a creative person shares an idea or dream, try to be encouraging!

Ideas need permission to succeed or fail on their own merit.

#10
The Perfect Swing

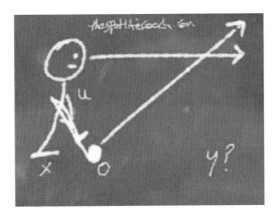

You are standing on the tee box. You can clearly see the green directly in front of you. A 165 yard par 3. The pin is placed perfectly in the center. A perfect day, a perfect distance, you select the perfect club, for the perfect shot, for this easy hole. You step up to address the ball, your three golfing partners are silent as you waggle, and then set your swing in motion.

You have the perfect swing!

You hit it great. It goes the perfect desired distance... but, about 50 yards to the left. You didn't shank it. You didn't pull it. You were simply lined up wrong.

Could your buddies see it?
Yes.

Could they have stopped you mid swing or before?
Yes.

Did you get mad that they didn't?
Maybe.

Did you ask them before you took your swing if you were lined up correctly?

No.

LIFE.

We may not need help with the swing. We may be tremendously gifted with the greatest swing. But if we are lined up wrong, what good is a perfect swing? We can be presented with the most perfect opportunity, under the perfect circumstances and yet if we are not 'lined up right', we will miss our target by 50 yards.

Don't waste your God given talent by not *lining up your life*. Don't be too proud or too good, or even afraid to ask for help in getting lined up right in your life.

#11
Perfectly Different

It seems the world is telling us that we are all the same, yet God tells us we are all different. I think it's well worth your time to inspect yourself.

HUH?

Notice how different you are from your brothers, sisters, friends, and well... Everyone! Hey, it's okay. In fact it's just right.
You were made different.

Think about it. You have your own fingerprint; like no one else EVER in the entire history of mankind! You have your own DNA... again, like no other!

Why?

Because, it takes us all to be a whole. We are all different parts of one big huge body. We are all designed to play a part.

YOU are made for a special purpose.

YOU are made different so others would need YOU and you would need others. So, if you aren't you...the rest of us are missing a part!

We all need each other.

God knows what He is doing. Trust Him and know you are specially made with specific gifts that we need to discover. Pay attention as to when, where, and how we are to use our gifts. It's like a life long detective show! Investigate, be aware, and figure it out.

What are your gifts?
How are you to use them?
Be different.
Be YOU.
(The rest of us are counting on it)

Romans 12: 3-8

#12
Foundation Vacation

Foundation Vacation

I love the beach. I love the mood people are in when they visit or live on the beach. I love the pace, the atmosphere, the sunrise, sunsets, salt water, waves and the *sand*.

Which got me thinking...

Matthew 7:24-27 (NIV)

[24] *"Therefore everyone who hears these words of mine and puts them into practice is like a wise man who built his house on the rock.* [25] *The rain came down, the streams rose, and the winds blew and beat against that house; yet it did not fall, because it had its foundation on the rock.* [26] *But everyone who hears these words of mine and does not put them into practice is like a foolish man who built his house on sand.* [27] *The rain came down, the streams rose, and the winds blew and beat against that house, and it fell with a great crash."*

I am certainly an observer. Living here at the beach I enjoy watching children and adults building sandcastles.

I began to think of the millions of sandcastles built upon this very beach over and over again. All washed away.

21

I began to think about my 'house', about me. My thoughts, plans, attitude, vision, relationships, job(s), and on and on... what are they built upon? Believe me, living at the beach will make anyone who is paying attention realize that it takes the tiniest of waves to destroy any foundation made of sand.

What are you building your house upon?

Are you building your life upon your sport, your workouts, your practice, or your performance?

I hope you get to the beach this summer and have a chance to really think about it.

#13
You're Surrounded

Surrounded

Whether you like it or not... you are surrounded.

Look around you.

Seriously, look around you.

What do you see?

What influences are surrounding you?
Who are the people you see?

What situation do you find yourself in?

Take the time to study your surroundings. Then ask yourself, is this what you wish to be in the middle of?

Do you feel caged by what you think you are *supposed* to act like or by things you are supposed to do?

Do you feel comforted by the support of right and good decisions that might go against the stereotypical expectations of others? What or who is influencing your decisions?

The answers to the questions above should tell you if you are surrounded by the right things.

How do your band members or teammates react when you know you are making right choices and those choices don't go along with things they might be doing?

Friends that are loyal, true, caring, trustworthy, and loving, will totally have your back no matter if you are making smart or right choices.

Being a good teammate or band member is difficult sometimes. Don't judge others...but, certainly use your judgment.

Don't be afraid to go against the grain of what society is saying a *rock star* or *famous athlete* should be like... or *how they should roll*. Don't justify your behavior due to your status as an athlete or musician/entertainer.

Be the difference.

The middle of the circle can change the entire surroundings of the circle.

#14
Do Something Difficult Everyday

Do something difficult every day.

What? Why would anyone do that? There's got to be an easier way... right? Are you always looking, searching for an easier way?

What do we learn from *easy*?

No one likes to start a workout but everyone likes to finish one. That is, if the workout is *difficult*. If the work out is easy then it doesn't matter, and if it doesn't matter, you are wasting your time. You get zero results and the lack of results will show up on game day!

Who are you?

Are you someone that looks for the easy way out resulting in laziness and a sedentary existence?

Or

Are you someone that takes on a challenge daily and searches for something that is difficult to do?

Choose difficult.

Choose challenges that push you.

Don't just apply this to practicing and working out.

Apply this to your life.

Is there someone you need to apologize to? That is very difficult to do, or so it often seems.

Is there someone you need to help?

Is there money you need to tithe or give?

Is there someone you need to serve and would doing so hard for you to do?

Do Something Difficult Every Day.

#15
Enjoy the Ride... and the Pizza

Have you ever heard anything like this?

"My son or daughter is going to be a great athlete! I am going to start training them in the womb! I have come up with a serious intense training schedule in their specialty sport ... I don't want them to fall behind others and not receive hundreds of offers and receive a college scholarship which would ruin my dreams."

I sure hope you are laughing! Okay, so you somehow KNOW and BELIEVE your child will play pro-sports, or at least gain a college scholarship. Maybe?

Note that the percentage of high school football players to go to the NCAA is 5.7%. That's not 5.7% on your team... that's 5.7% of ALL High School Players.

Now that's just talking about High School. What about entry level organized sports for kids? Really? Who cares?

HAVE FUN!

Again, I hope you are laughing.

The National Collegiate Athletic Association (NCAA) has compiled the following chart that estimates the probability of high school athletes competing in college athletics.

Athletes	Women's Basketball	Men's Basketball	Baseball	Men's Ice Hockey	Football	Men's soccer
High School Athletes	452,929	546,335	470,671	36,263	1,071,775	358,935
High School senior athletes	129,408	156,096	134,477	10,361	306,221	102,553
NCAA Athletes	15,096	16,571	28,767	3,973	61,252	19,797
NCAA Freshman Positions	4,313	4,735	8,219	1,135	17,501	5,655
NCAA Senior Athletes	3,355	3,682	6,393	883	13,612	4,398
NCAA Senior Athletes Drafted	32	44	600	33	250	75
Percentage: High School To NCAA	3.3%	3.0%	6.1%	11.0%	5.7%	5.5%
Percentage: NCAA To Professional	1.0%	1.2%	9.4%	3.7%	1.8%	1.7%
Percentage: High School To Professional	0.02%	0.03%	0.45%	0.32%	0.08%	

CHALK TALK

Perspective and Balance is key here. We should keep in mind that a few of these kids don't even know if they won or lost after they play their games. They are just excited to ride in the car or van with you and their buddies on the way to eat Pizza!

Keep in mind it is about *the ride...* the beginning of a wonderful journey.

So enjoy the ride with your kids (and enjoy the pizza). There's a 5.7% chance of playing college football and a 100% chance of them enjoying a pizza after a game in youth football!

#16
Playing Position

Playing Position

What is playing position? I've heard it a million times; coaches barking out; "*Get yourself in playing position!*"

It's your stance. It's your foundation up; feet to brain readiness.

I had a coach that would describe it like this; He wanted to see a Z in your knees. A flat back... 1/4 squat, feet shoulder width apart, head up. He wanted you braced, ready to react, respond, and move. He wanted your body in position for being keenly alert and ready for anything.

Are you in playing position for life?

Maybe you're not. Maybe you're standing tall and proud with your feet comfortably close together. You are easily rocked, tipped off balance, or knocked down.

CHALK TALK

Maybe you're looking down, not paying attention. Maybe you aren't aware of your surroundings or you choose to ignore them. You will be easily blind-sided.

Maybe you are always day dreaming about easier ways of doing things and you aren't recognizing the opportunities that are directly in front of you.

You will be easily passed by and left standing wondering why things aren't working out for you.

Get yourself in playing position.
Ready yourself for this day, this time.
Be in the moment and <u>play hard</u>!
It's more fun to live life in playing position!

#17
Public Speaking Requires Public Listening

What good is a speaker that doesn't listen?

As a songwriter I learned a long time ago to observe. Observe not only by sight, but also by listening. How many song ideas do songwriter's get from a phrase we hear someone say? How many songs come from a twist on a word we hear, or from our own take on a person's story we hear?

We don't wake up in the morning and talk all day! If we did there would be little to write about.

Writers must listen.

As I have begun to be blessed with opportunity to be a keynote speaker I can *see* that the key to speaking in public is *listening*!

Speakers must listen.

What?

Listening is a great way to observe and learn *truth*. Learning the truth of what is on both the surface and underneath the surface of what is really going on in peoples lives; joy, hurt, pain, struggle, confusion, desires, direction, routines, habits, focus, and on and on. Listening allows you to respond correctly.

Speaking and talking is great, and yes, it's very important.

No one is more a *Keynote Speaker* than YOU.

When we speak out loud we are all public speakers. But, we need to always consider that we also need to be public listeners to better speak!

It's a twister, right? Are you talking more or listening?

So think about it. Try to talk less around your groups of friends. And *listen* to them.

Try to talk less in your one on one conversations, and *listen* to whose talking to you.

If you do... I bet you will have better things to say.

James 1:19 (NIV)
[19] *My dear brothers and sisters, take note of this: Everyone should be quick to listen, slow to speak and slow to become angry.*

#18
Born Leaders

What are you looking for in a leader? What type of person do you want to follow? What message is the leader you are following showing?

We are all influenced by someone, especially at a young age. Our early years of playing sports are filled with those that we wish to mirror. Asking a young player why they like a particular collegiate or professional player is always interesting to me. I get answers that vary from;

I like their uniform.
They are cool.
I like the dance they do after they sack someone... or score a touchdown.
I like their number.

The answers are fairly typical of a young persons impression from watching a player live or on TV. Of course none of these answers reflect in any way, someone being a true 'leader'; yet... they are being followed.

Seriously think about that.

CHALK TALK

They are being followed for reasons that seem silly to most of us. Someone is watching. And it's not just athletic events in which players are watched. It's their personal lives as well.

I am very familiar with athlete's that say up front that they are not comfortable with being a *leader* just because they play a sport. I admire and respect that honesty a great deal. But being a leader doesn't really have *an opt* out option.

Let me explain.
If you are a father... you are a leader.
If you are a mother... you are a leader.
If you are a brother, sister, uncle, aunt, granddad, grandma, neighbor, friend, classmate, roommate, teacher, coach, preacher, or _____.

WE ARE ALL LEADERS of some type.

Someone is watching us.
We will *lead* those that are watching us by whatever we do; good, bad, or ugly.
We don't have a choice to opt out.
We are going to be an influence no matter what we do.

What kind of leader are you?

#19
Your Face is on You

We cannot control much can we? Think about it.

From the time we get up until we go to bed daily, there is little we can control. Someone may cut in front of us in traffic. The sink might surprise you with a leak. The neighbor might leave their kids toys in your driveway. Your boss might show up in an ill mood and threaten to fire everybody. Your coach may decide today is the day he is going to do the drill that everyone hates... and then announce two more hours of watching tape. You may find your name moved down on the roster for starting position. Your history exam is the same day as your physics exam. Your significant other breaks up with you just after you bought them the *perfect* gift.

There is really nothing we can do to control these things. Why do we try so hard to change things we cannot change? We spend hours and hours trying to get out of things, change things, and rearrange things to get the result we would rather have.

Stop. Concentrate on what we can change; things like your *face* or your *attitude!*

Think about this: your face usually directly reflects your attitude. We are in total control of our attitudes, therefore, we are in total control over our faces! No one can make you change it, rearrange it, or cause you to have a different result with it.

Your face is on YOU.
Choose wisely.

I love this following verse. It's so simple and very easy to understand.

Philippians 2:14 (NIV)
14 Do everything without grumbling or arguing"

Everything. *Everything = Attitude*
Who wants to be around a grumbling and argumentative person?
Control what you can.
Choose your face. That's on you.

#20
What are you Fishing for?

I love to fish. I think most people love to fish.
The fact is, whether or not we realize it... we are all fishing! What do I mean by that?

Consider this: what decision process do we go through when we are baiting our hook for the particular fish we would like to catch. First, you must familiarize yourself with what the particular fish you are fishing for might be attracted to.

For instance, Catfish and Carp are bottom-dwellers. Therefore, they seem to prefer bait that is scented like worms, chicken livers, sometimes hotdogs, and cheese. Bass prefer minnows or frogs that move in the water or an injured prey. So, you might have to manipulate the bait a bit and that could be even more impressive than the bait you choose.

So, I ask you to consider this; look around you... Look at yourself.

What are you wearing?
How do you dress?

Do you wear clothes and/or make-up in a way that might attract the very thing you are fishing for? Or are you wearing the things that might attract what you are NOT fishing for?

What words are coming out of your mouth?

Are you speaking in a positive way?

Are you always complaining or grumbling?

Do your words attract the response that you are fishing for?

How do you treat other people?

Are your actions towards others attracting the type of friends you wish to be around?

What type of attitude do you show daily?

Does your attitude shine?

Does your response to difficult situations reflect your response to delightful situations?

Does the attitude you are projecting reflect the attitude you are finding yourself surrounded by?

Are you attracting what you are fishing for?

Maybe it's time to switch the bait you are using for something that attracts the type of 'fish' you are fishing for. When you look into the body of water you are fishing in, notice your reflection. What do you see?

Luke 5:6 (NIV)

6 When they had done so, they caught such a large number of fish that their nets began to break.

#21
Two Steps Forward and One Step Back

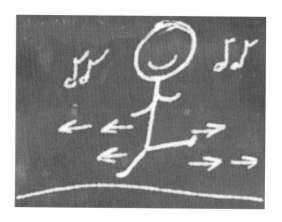

"Two steps forward and one step back"
or
"One step forward and two steps back"

I have heard this anecdote used both ways. Either way, it's meaning is to express the frustration of making great efforts and getting nowhere. I choose a different outlook. Please consider these two things I am terrible at:

Patience
Math

I acknowledge and recognize the frustration in both areas. I also see commonality in both sayings. Or maybe I *choose* to see the *positive* commonality in both sayings.

Patience is needed to maintain a positive outlook when we feel we are trying hard and it seems the harder we try, we still find our goal seems to be further away than when we started.

We hit set-backs.

CHALK TALK

We hit walls.
We get knocked down.
We get discouraged.
We carry a load that seemingly gets heavier and harder to bear.

Have patience.

Each anecdote requires some math (and for me, a calculator) to figure out in 365 days how many steps forward vs. how many steps backwards one would actually take? And of course which anecdote you choose to plug the correct forwards vs. backwards steps into the equation to get your final number.

I'm not worried about the final number. I am only concerned with the first step. I choose to see each anecdote *mathematically* as numbers in motion.

One, two, three... one, two, three...
Sounds musical to me. Sounds like a dance to me!
As long as there is a 'ONE', that means you are starting... it means you are trying... and it means you are not quitting! It means you are at least *walking* and if you choose, you are *dancing*!

We can hear the music behind our struggles if we choose to. Don't forget in each anecdote there is always a *step forward*. ALWAYS.

So don't quit.
Keep taking that first step.
Keep walking on!
Dance.

2 Corinthians 5:7 (ESV)
⁷ for we walk by faith, not by sight.

#22
Knock – Knock… Whose There?

How many times have we heard people say, *Opportunity is knocking?*
Really?
When does opportunity ever knock?

Never.
Opportunity doesn't seek you.
Opportunity doesn't come calling on you.
It doesn't tap, ring, knock or pound on your door.

Don't be mislead by this phrase that perhaps gets overused.
Don't be tricked into waiting around for your *opportunity.*

Don't sit idle.

Don't be lazy waiting for an opportunity to knock!
It won't.
We have to knock on opportunity!
That's right.

We must *get up, get out, work, then work some more.*
We must *develop skills, trades, senses, awareness with wisdom.*
We must *train, practice, rehearse, with patience and aggressiveness.*

CHALK TALK

We must *take chances, be prepared, be keen, always studying while being very aware... we must take action.*
What are you doing now?
Think about the way you are living.

THINK ABOUT;
Your *manners, morals, ethics, principals, integrity.*
Think about all of the things mentioned above.
You will find your doors of opportunity at the end of this path.

Knock On!

#23
Tomorrow, Today, Tonight, Too Late

How many times have you made a New Years Resolution? How many times has your resolution been the same resolution you made the year before, or the years before?

It's very easy to put off work, tasks, assignments, papers due, homework, etc. But what about the things you wish for... or long for?

Your <u>someday</u> *I am going to be* ____
Your <u>one day</u> *I am going to become* ____
"Tomorrow is a new day and that will be the day I begin."
"Yes! I will start tomorrow!"

I don't know about you, but I have had many, many of these *tomorrows*. And those kinds of tomorrows come and go *fast*.

*T*omorrow nights found me not feeling so hot about *to*days activities. Tomorrow nights found me at times depressed and dejected due to my lack of diligence, work, laziness and commitment to my *Tomorrow* which became *today*... turning into *tonight* and crashing on **too late**!

Have you ever blown your chance?

CHALK TALK

Can you get over a 'tomorrow' opportunity that came and went?
Sure you can!
But, not sitting around saying, "I'll start tomorrow."

START NOW

This year is going to be an awesome year for you!
High Jump your Rainbow.

Don't let *tomorrow* turn into *too late*.

#24
We Need Heroes!

We Need Heroes

Here's how Dictionary.com defines the word:

Heroes - he ro[heer-oh] noun, plural he roes;
 1. a man of distinguished courage or ability, admired for his brave deeds and noble qualities.
 2. a person who, in the opinion of others, has heroic qualities or has performed a heroic act and is regarded as a model or ideal: He was a local hero when he saved the drowning child.

WE NEED HEROES

I have heard some say recently that we don't need heroes. What is wrong with a hero? When we were small children did we not all have someone that we considered a hero? What is wrong with having a hero?

Well... therein lies the rub. It all depends on whom you choose to be your *hero*. It is key here to recognize the word, *choose*.
When left up to us to decide, who we pick to be our hero, we don't always pick the best choice to 'save' us or for us to try to model ourselves after.

CHALK TALK

Heroes. Without heroes, without leaders, without mentors we are all really lost sheep. I have been a lost sheep. I did not find any comfort in being lost. Lost means alone. I looked for a hero. I wished to be saved by a hero.

I am more comfortable in a group of friends, a family, or a herd. Discovering that makes me realize I also recognize the need for a Shepherd.

Check out Dictionary.com's definition of a Shepherd:

Shepherd- *shep ·herd* [shep-erd] noun
1. a person who herds, tends, and guards sheep.
2. a person who protects, guides, or watches over a person or group of people.
3. a member of the clergy.
4. the Shepherd, Jesus Christ.

Heroes are among us all. Look at the definition again. Think about your mom, your dad. Think about your coach. Think about those that take time with you to teach you, to mentor you. They most likely aren't wearing a cape or a mask. But they swoop in when you are nearing trouble or you are in trouble and they SAVE you.

Is it hard to imagine a Shepherd being a hero? We often choose strangers, people that do not know us as our heroes. Those that do not know us nor do they care a single thing about us.

BUT.
If you are a lost sheep, and there are many wolves around...
You need a HERO:
A good Shepherd.

John 10:11(NIV)
"I am the good shepherd. The good shepherd lays down his life for the sheep. (12) The hired hand is not the shepherd and does not own the sheep. So when he sees the wolf coming, he abandons the sheep and runs away. Then the wolf attacks the flock and scatters it. (13) The man runs away because he is a hired hand and cares nothing for the sheep.

BRYAN KENNEDY

We need heroes.
We need the good Shepherd.

#25
Love to Walk?

Love to walk?

A baby has a walk (wobbly for sure... they walk like their feet aren't expecting to touch the ground with each step).

A toddler has a walk (they really don't walk... they run. When they do walk they usually are holding the hand of a grown up walking).

A teenager has a walk (they walk with some sort of identity to their newly discovered or desired personality... it changes).

A young man has a walk (he walks with eagerness. A pace that is ready to be where they are headed)

A young lady has a walk (She walks with respect and awareness of all around them). A football player has a walk, a basketball player has a walk, a soccer player, tennis, hockey.

Think about it. Think of those you know playing different

sports. They all have a certain walk... don't they? We all do.

Think about this: A Christian has a walk.
2 John 1:6 (NIV)

⁶ And this is love: that we walk in obedience to his commands. As you have heard from the beginning, his command is that you walk in love.

Walking is good for us all... and God *loves* a good walk. :)

#26
Don't Just Keep Your Eye on the Ball

We can all be looking at the same thing, but it is what we see that makes us different. Some things are more commonly *seen* than others.

A center field Home Run is easy to see as the ball clears the fence. We all look at a game on TV and most of us watch the ball. But, there is so much more to see.

What do you see when you look at a football game? Do you just keep your eyes on the ball? Or, do you watch the offensive line, the pulling guard, the nose tackle linebacker stunt, or the free safety blitz?

What do you see?
Most people watch the ball.
Most people have little idea of the chess pieces moving around the field during a 5 second play.
They only see the ball.

And they could be missing the game... or you could be missing the heart of the game.

Life is like this.

We do it with people.

We see their lives as the ball.

We watch them and see if they are advancing the ball in their lives, or if they fumble, throw an interception or have to kick (punt).

In other words, we notice if they score or don't score. What we don't see is *their practice,* their lives, what made them run the plays they run.

We don't see what their coaches are or were like. We don't see what type of work ethic they have been taught or maybe not taught at all. We don't see their training regiment and we don't get to listen in to their chalk talks. We only see their performance, or, the score!

Next time you are talking to a friend, a loved one... or even someone you just met on a plane, a bus, or in the bleachers, think about what you are seeing. Then take a second to think about what you cannot see; what everyone else is not focusing on... and see if you can see the bigger picture of what is before you.

All God's pictures are BIG

And, God loves the details in each picture... each person. It takes a lot of time, coaching, experience, practicing, and repetition to be who you are.

It takes a lot of time, coaching, experience, practicing and repetition for us to see others without just focusing on the obvious. In this case... don't just keep your eye on the ball.

#27
Be-Live What You Know

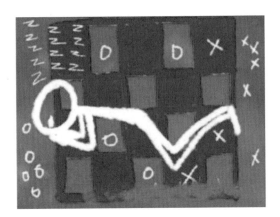

So you have come up with a strategy. You have finally come up with a plan! That's exciting!

Maybe you have just seen or heard a really motivating 'chalk talk'? Your vision is clear and you now are positive in your direction and goal. That is awesome! All of your senses are peaked and you are mentally and emotionally fired up! Just writing about it fires me up!

Now, let me ask you this question; What are YOU going to do about it? That's right...

What are you going to do about it?

You see, even though you may have come slowly to understand what it is you should be doing.

What is it you need to be doing?
What ARE YOU going to do about it?
We can have the vision, the plan, the motivation, the emotional rush of great intentions, but we still have to take action.
It is NOT enough to believe in what we know.
We must BE - LIVE what we know.
We must *be* it.

And

We must *live* it.
BE LIVE IT

Consider this from **James 2:14-24 (NIV):**
"Show me your faith without deeds, and I will show you my faith by my deeds."
Faith relates to what we might call our vision: our motivation.

We get all fired up when we discover our new vision and clear direction, but if we do not participate in it, it is nothing.
You can tell your coach, your teacher, your parents and yourself about your new vision and wonderful intentions, but if you do not *work* or participate in that vision, well… you are all talk.

BE_LIVE what you know.
Be it… **And**… Live it.

#28
Know Your No

No.
Learn to say it.
Learn to use it.
KNOW your NO.

And *Positively (+) Know* that your *No* doesn't need to be explained.

The word '*No*' is defined by The Merriam-Webster Dictionary;
No- **adverb** \ '**n**☐ \
—*used to give a negative answer or reply to a question, request, or offer: in a way that shows a negative response*

    This word is basically defined as a *negative* word. And by true definition it is indeed. Our ears have become conditioned so that when we hear the word we associate negative thoughts/things upon the word falling on our ears.

NO!

    Most likely this begins to be a *trained* negative word from our very beginnings. Some of our mom's and dad's have often said *no* in a calm and normal voice, occasionally delivered with a smile. But, other times some might deliver the word with another voice that comes from what seems to be some sort of alien from another planet... and loud!

"NO"!

Dog trainers will tell you the first word a dog should learn is *no*. We associate this word with being denied the chance to explore. We associate this word with ruining our good time ahead.
The word means exactly as The Merriam-Webster Dictionary defines it, but believe me, it would be a mistake to view this word as always being a *negative* word.

The word *no* can be the most positive word in your entire vocabulary! Yes the word no can be the most positive word you ever use! It might even save your life.

When we use this word after being offered to participate in something negative... it becomes a very positive word. Everyone has heard *just say no to drugs*. No is a great word in that situation. And the coolest thing about this word is... it needs no reason *why*. It might need to be repeated, but it needs no reason why. *No* period. That's it. That's enough.

Someone not wishing to have their hand held... or to be kissed by someone... and so on. *No*. This is a positive word used here. When others asks us or attempt to persuaded us to go places, do things, or even BE things that we do not feel comfortable with... No.

You have to know your *no*.
Know where you draw your *no* line.
Don't be afraid to use this word to free you from a situation you do not feel comfortable with.

Saying no can be the most positive thing you ever say in your entire life. Don't be afraid to use it. There is no such thing as losing a friend when you choose the word **no** when asked to say **yes** to something you **know** is wrong.

CHALK TALK

Know Your No.
And don't be afraid to let others know it too.
No need to offer a why.

Matthew 5:37 (NIV)

[37] *All you need to say is simply 'Yes' or 'No'; anything beyond this comes from the evil one.*

#29
Wit + Strength

A 320lb pulling guard that doesn't pull = 0
A QB that can throw a rope 75 yards that cannot identify the Mike Linebacker = 0

Wit... *(the power of reasoning)*. Wit alone is a powerful tool. It is a necessary tool. *Wit* is taught everywhere and in every place. It is always praised!

Strength is also a powerful tool. Yet... it seems to be taught and praised less and less... or at least, last to be recognized. It seems to be frowned upon in certain circles. Perhaps due to the reputation it might get from the stereotypical *meat head* portrayed in movies, the 'dumb' football player etc. This is a shame.

Wit and Strength, are needed equally. Both should be recognized. We tend to accept wit or *smart* thinking we see in a person. But sometimes it seems that we discourage the *strength* we see in someone especially if they are athletic in appearance.

But, strength comes in other shapes and forms; *courage, bravery, fortitude, determination, relentless effort, backbone, toughness.* We all know a person cannot rely upon muscles and brawn to accomplish all in life! Of course a person MUST use their wit.

But, just as strength requires thinking, thinking requires strength to be most effective. No one should rely upon their wit alone. They must call upon strength as well. And you don't have to be a hulking giant to have strength.

Consider this story as an example:

1 Samuel 17 (NIV)
David and Goliath
Wit & Strength
vs.
Strength

This battle is not won by *wit* alone and it certainly wasn't won by *strength* alone. But it is key to note that it was LOST by strength alone!

So... Get your *wit's* about you and s*trengthen* up!

#30
It's all about Verse 27

It's All About You...?   Maybe, if it's all about you doing some of the following;

Do something good.
Do something embarrassingly good.
Do something that maybe most would not do.
Do something that might require you to go out on a limb.
Do something you don't have time for.
Do something that is inconvenient.
Do something you might get laughed at for doing.
Do something that will impact someone else forever.
Do something one out of three would do!

In other words...
Be a good neighbor.

Luke 10:25-37 (NIV)
The Parable of the Good Samaritan

[25] *On one occasion an expert in the law stood up to test Jesus. "Teacher," he asked, "what must I do to inherit eternal life?"*

26 "What is written in the Law?" he replied. "How do you read it?"
27 He answered, "'Love the Lord your God with all your heart and with all your soul and with all your strength and with all your mind'[a]; and, 'Love your neighbor as yourself.'[b]"
28 "You have answered correctly," Jesus replied. "Do this and you will live."
29 But he wanted to justify himself, so he asked Jesus, "And who is my neighbor?"
30 In reply Jesus said: "A man was going down from Jerusalem to Jericho, when he was attacked by robbers. They stripped him of his clothes, beat him and went away, leaving him half dead. 31 A priest happened to be going down the same road, and when he saw the man, he passed by on the other side. 32 So too, a Levite, when he came to the place and saw him, passed by on the other side. 33 But a Samaritan, as he traveled, came where the man was; and when he saw him, he took pity on him. 34 He went to him and bandaged his wounds, pouring on oil and wine. Then he put the man on his own donkey, brought him to an inn and took care of him. 35 The next day he took out two denarii[c] and gave them to the innkeeper. 'Look after him,' he said, 'and when I return, I will reimburse you for any extra expense you may have.'
36 "Which of these three do you think was a neighbor to the man who fell into the hands of robbers?"
37 The expert in the law replied, "The one who had mercy on him."
Jesus told him, "Go and do likewise."

When we do likewise it changes our lives in enormous ways. So, it's not "all about that bass", or putting your left foot in and taking your left foot out and doing the Hokey-Pokey and it's not all about you and it's not all about me.

It's all about you AND me doing likewise.
It's all about verse 27!

61

#31
The Truth About Shortcuts

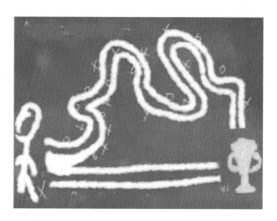

It doesn't come wrapped. It doesn't always make a grand entrance, it doesn't change itself to fit any convenience or circumstance. If there were anything that ever exactly defines the phrase *it is what it is*... it's TRUTH.

Truth is never manufactured, packaged, or shipped.
Truth is always the same.
Truth has no intentions.
Truth has no agenda.
Truth needs no votes.
Truth doesn't have a click or club or gang.
Truth runs from no thing or person.
Truth is right without being prideful.

We spend hours days and sometimes our lives trying to bend, shape, re-shape, hide, run, change, reflect, deflect and change the truth. In other words we will travel around the world to avoid it!

Shortcuts.

CHALK TALK

Let's talk about shortcuts. We don't want or feel like doing 100 sit-ups daily for the rest of our lives... so we try some new *As seen of TV* device that *guarantee's* us great abs in 5 minutes. We look for, desire, and welcome what appears to be a shortcut. We want to lose 5 or 10 pounds. Instead of eating great healthy foods regularly we go for the crazy Hercules Beach Zeus and Athena high intake Greek God liquid protein veggie fruit and steak diet. We welcome the shortcut. We seem to always look for the shortcut. They are so appealing...

Except when it comes to the truth!

Think about all the time we waste. The energy it takes to skirt around the truth as we try to avoid it.

I do it.
You do it.
We all do it.

Think about the people we hurt, including ourselves trying to avoid the short cut of just dealing with the Truth. This topic is a hard one for me to write because as I think about these words I find myself wanting to *avoid* the short cut. I find myself wanting to maybe *delete* this blog and write another so that I don't have to deal with this subject myself!
but...

I will choose to take this short cut... this is a good short cut.
I will think about, realize, face and deal with my truths.
They aren't going to change no matter how I try to change them or avoid them. Yours will not either.

So avoid the 'made for TV' short cuts. Let's choose the short cut to the truth. It saves a lot of time, energy, pain, and causes us to miss out on so many blessings. Truth might seem to be the enemy to us at times. It might be the last thing we want to hear or even know. Getting to the truth helps us. It's the one good time to take a *shortcut*.

John 8:32 (NIV)

[32] *Then you will know the truth, and the truth will set you free."*

And that's the truth.

#32
Defining U

"Who are you... who who, who who?"

It's a really great song, and a really great question. How often does this happen to you?

"Hi...
Nice to meet you…
Do you play sports?
What position do you play?"

Then more questions asking if you are a starter... play a lot... what grade, what year... etc. The answers to these questions provide the person asking the question with information that immediately helps to 'label' or 'define' you.

As a Life Coach I would like to ask you this: does the sport/position/instrument you play define you? Does your talent define you?

We all have Twitter accounts, Instagram accounts, Facebook... etc.
Social Networks. Social Networking…
Do they define you? Do the number of Likes you have on your fan

page define you? How about the number of Likes you get on one of your posts? How about the comments you get on a photo?
Stop and think about these things.

What is it that defines you?

Your gifts are often the first thing someone recognizes, and they are the first things someone uses to define you. That is normal. We should celebrate our gifts! We should enjoy our gifts.
God gave them to us, specifically to each of us for a reason.
But we should be careful not to let these amazing gifts take over our lives so that our foundation becomes based upon these gifts.

Our foundation *should be* based solidly upon the *gift giver*!
That is sure fire formula for keeping your head on straight, staying humble, while at the same time, getting out there and ROCKING the world with your specific gifts!

Don't hide them.
Use them.
But... don't let them define you or control you.
Don't let your gift be who you are. Know that the gift giver is the reason you are who you are.

John 3:16 (NIV)

16 For God so loved the world that he gave his one and only Son, that whoever believes in him shall not perish but have eternal life.

#33
Confidence in Weakness?

Would you agree that Peyton Manning was confident as a quarterback that he could throw a forty-yard strike to a receiver running across the middle? Would you agree that Lebron James is confident that he can dunk a basketball? Of course!

Think about this: can we be confident in our weaknesses? The answer to that is... Yes!

It is very important for us to recognize our gifts! It is very important for us to know where our strengths are. It is very important for us to be confident with them!

However, we should also recognize our weaknesses and be confident with them!

What?

It's like this...
We all have strengths.
We all have weaknesses.

Say for example your gift is communication. You are able to get a point across with clarity. The listener sees your point and understands exactly what you intended. They feel motivated, clear and precise after hearing or reading your words. Be confident and communicate on!

You may not have a gift for building. You cannot even open a Lego box. Some would consider your 'non-gift' for building as a weakness. Now think about this; I say be confident in your lack of ability to build!

Again…what?

No, I don't mean you should brag about not being gifted in building nor do I mean do not ever build or help someone build! I mean if you are called upon to build… Tell people you cannot! Tell them that isn't your strength!

Again…
Please offer to help them. Tell them you are willing to learn. Please volunteer if you feel led to do so.

BUT…
Don't feel like you *have to be a builder.*
Let those gifted in building build!
You communicate.

You see we all need to be confident in our gifts
and be confident in our weaknesses too! God designed us to be that way.

Reference Romans 12 and 1 Corinthians 12

#34
Level the Playing Field

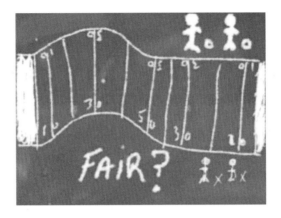

We've got to *level the playing field.*

People love to use sports analogies to make a point outside of sports.

"Hit it out of the park."
"Swinging for the fence."
"It was a slam dunk."

Now we have the popular; *We have to level the playing field.* What does this mean? What does it mean to you? It basically is meant to mean; we have to make this fair for everybody... right? But, it seems that it has come to mean the following:

1. Everybody should play
2. Everybody should win
3. Everybody should get a trophy
4. No one gets hurt
5. It all ends in a tie

Sounds fair... and that makes us feel good. Two teams compete on the same playing field, right? The teams swap sides at the quarters, halves, and periods... even tennis players swap sides. So, wouldn't this be *fair?*

Bottom line is this: don't fall for the *level the playing field line.* In fact, prepare yourself for an unleveled playing field in life because... well, it's unleveled!

Do not allow yourself to think someone is going to make it fair for you. Don't wait to play until the field is level. Don't wait for your parents, coaches, organizations, or your boss to make your life fair because no matter how level the field of play is, IT'S NOT ALWAYS FAIR.

There is someone bigger.
There is someone stronger.
There is someone faster.
There is someone tougher.
There is someone that has a better coach, opportunity, shoes, weight room, neighborhood, and on and on and on.

AND... there are others who are just *better.*

Want to know what makes the playing field level or unleveled? People. You see PEOPLE determine the field of play. People make a difference no matter what the playing field's level is.

YOU make a difference.
YOU determine the outcome not the playing field!
Don't worry about your field of play.
Don't let your circumstances determine your outcome.
We've all heard games are won and loss in the kicking game...

Kick *circumstances* butt.

Concentrate on the best you can be and the best you can do. Welcome the challenge of an unleveled playing field! Don't let the field of play be an excuse!

#35

First String Parents

What if your child doesn't start?
What if your child doesn't make 1st string?
What if your child doesn't make 2nd string?
What if your child gets moved to a position you don't think they should play or YOU don't want them to play?

What if your child is being coached in a way that you obviously *know* is not the best, and you certainly without a doubt instruct and coach better? What if your child gets cut from the team?

Wow.

I have heard of parents moving their entire families, uprooting their entire lives, leaving their jobs, family and friends in order to insure their child is a starter after their child gets labeled *2nd String*. They cannot imagine their child being 2nd. They cannot accept 2nd string for their child. They know their child should be a star and should be starting no matter their experience, age or ability or the others on the team.

So, they will do whatever it takes to find a place, a school, and a coach that will make sure their child IS a starter and a star... (or at least has the appearance of being one).

Most of you will reading will fall in to one of three categories:

1. You are thinking; "That sounds crazy"! "What kind of parent would do something like that?"
2. "Ouch! I have had some of those exact thoughts. I have to admit I have been tempted to do something like that."
3. "What in the *bleep* is wrong with that? Any parent that loves their kid would and should do just that"!

We have seen all of these types of responses if we have/had a child participating in organized sports... beginning at the age of three. You might ask me what is the proper way to respond to your child not getting to start or play. Well, I don't know how you should respond. I would ask you to think IF you are thinking of your child, or if you are thinking of YOU?

Being brutally honest ask yourself these questions:

Am I thinking about me?
Am I embarrassed?
Will this effect my bragging at the office or in the grocery store, etc.?
Does this make me feel a bit left out going to the games since my son/daughter is not playing?
Am I not as proud?
Am I not as 'important' amongst my co-workers and friends?

Everyone wants their child to start. Everyone wants their child to have the best! The truth is that for most of our lives we are not in control over our 'playing position'. Think of all the jobs you have had or will have. We have hundreds of coaches, bosses, and assistant coaches. We can't always be first string. We certainly don't always *start*.

So, the question becomes "what do you do when you don't make the first team?" How do you answer that question? What are you teaching your child by your actions and reactions? We can ask questions all day about what do we do if our child doesn't start or play... Maybe think more about these questions;

What do you do if your child doesn't try?
What do you do if your child quits?

Be a parent. Teach and encourage the mentality of never quitting because of circumstances.

You are first string parents... always!

#36
Father's Day's

I am not a father. I have no qualifications for knowing anything about being a father other than being a godfather to a wonderful teenage girl and a step dad to my lovely wife's son. Then there is the fact that I myself am a son, and that along with my years of paying great attention... making notes and observing, all the while listening and having thousands of conversations with many of you biological fathers everywhere.

All that to say, my purpose for this blog is to make a humble attempt to maybe set at ease the minds of many of you fathers out there that are struggling at times with your son(s). (And I say *sons* purposefully omitting daughters).

I have a simple statement I wish to share. I would like for you to consider this statement and keep tucked away in your thoughts and hearts as fatherhood takes you down an often, tumultuous, path. Here it is:

It is in every young man's journey to find fault with his father.

That's right. This is my observation. I have observed this to be some sort of natural way or path to ease the *disconnect* as the son begins the journey pulling away to find a path of his own. A path that most times he will go to great lengths to make different from his father's path.

Think about it.
All the disagreements.
All the anger.
And all the grunts, sighs, and scowled brows.
All the dead silence.

Somehow it's natural.
Somehow perhaps it's necessary?

I don't get personal here too much. But, I will on this. I said above that *it is in every young man's journey to find fault with his father.* Boy, I did mine. I searched and I found. It's not hard to find fault with your father, in fact... it's easy.

He's just a man, like me, like you.
I was quick and eager to find fault with my father and began to become slower to find the greatness in my father.

I pulled and pulled and pulled away from him. I have two brothers. We are all different yet we have the same dad. And all of us pulled away from our father. Someone we love very much.

Why?

Maybe just maybe it's a young boy's way of dealing with the inevitable *Break Up* that lies before him. He must leave his father and become a man. Not like his dad. Not like his brother(s). His own man.

Here is the deal:

How hard must this process be for you dad's to have a son you love so much and know this to be true.
And you put up with it.
You bite your lip.
You allow it.

And, what if you have more than one son? You allow each to be there own man and take the pulling away from you in the individual way they each choose to pick out the faults they find in you.

Father's Day's **are tough.**

God bless you dads.

God bless your patience.

God bless your wisdom and your faults.
I love my dad very much.
Yes I once was a boy picking and finding his every fault.
Now I am a man thanking God for my dad. The good, the bad, and the incredibly great!
I am a son who loves his father.

Happy Father's Day's Dad's.

#37
Big Talkers

We all have seen them. We all have heard them.
Big Talkers.

They can be found in most any sport and in most any locker room. They sleek through our schools in the hallways and they make themselves known in the holding areas on recruiting trips. They are loud in the dorm rooms, lunchrooms and classes all over.
Big Talkers know their every stat. They know every article they are mentioned in. And *they will* tell you all about it. They can tell you every school that is recruiting them and most of what they say grows with each new set of ears listening.

Leaders? Often times they are also *big talkers* but, the life of their *leadership* is often short lived.

You see, most big talkers are natural leaders. Why? Because weak followers are suckers for big talk. You see those that pay attention to big talkers and buy into a big talkers... talk... Well, some of those listeners find themselves in some sort of shock & *awe*. Sometimes they are even fearful, other times they are intimidated, and all of this by mere words and usually a well rehearsed dynamic presentation.

We are all eager to believe in magic!

Then there is another type of leader.

What about the NO Talkers and the KNOW Talkers?
Let's call them *know* Talkers, the ones that just *know*. They don't see a
need to talk, or if they do, they don't see a need to talk big.
Their confidence is strong. And talking about their selves, well, it
serves no purpose. They let their actions speak for them.

Think for a moment:

> Who are you following?
> How are you leading?

In case you haven't noticed this in your own life... begin to pay
attention to this fact. NOTHING, I repeat NOTHING speaks
louder than a person's actions. This holds true in every situation I can
think of.

You can be loud and talk big and lead most for a short time.
Eventually your actions will catch up with your words and you will be
left with leading a very small few.

OR

You can be quiet, speak when needed, and let your extraordinary
actions, hard work, and consistency speak at a volume that will lead
others for a long time!

You see the big talkers lead the small people, people that follow
because they like what they hear. More than often the big talkers do
not deliver. Their actions are rarely as grandiose as their voices.

Ecclesiastes 9:7 (NIV)
*[17] The quiet words of the wise are more to be heeded
than the shouts of a ruler of fools.*

#38
Run/Walk with Forgiveness

Do you run, jog, or walk? Where? **What surface or foundation is underneath you?**

Before I began traveling for work on a world tour, I found a new trail to run on near where I was staying in Tennessee. It is a beautiful track that offers the most picturesque views that the rolling hills of middle Tennessee can offer. This trail is actually a horse pasture that was converted into a city park of sorts, open to the public.

Should you know anything about me at all, you will know that I feel right at home in the middle of a horse pasture. So, it makes perfect sense that this trail is one of my all time favorites to jog on. More quickly to my point today; running in a horse pasture is a great place to learn forgiveness.

Forgiveness?

What does running in a horse pasture have to do with forgiveness? Keep in mind my new found horse pasture/walking, jogging, running trail no longer has any horses or any sort of livestock roaming anywhere on it. But, since I grew up there, I know first hand they were there for many years.

The pasture still consists of old barns, implement sheds, and a couple of old silos. And of course, the land on which the horses grazed.

Now, if you have never been in a pasture you might not be aware that horses walking or running leave some pretty decent sized divots in the ground. These divots are different from those caused by a golfer. These divots do not dig underneath the ground exposing the soil or sand, no these are more like hidden camouflaged, sunk in, fairly deep impressions that are very hard to see until you step in or near one. And when you do step in one you can easily roll your ankle and cause instant pain or serious injury.
(In addition to what the horse's hooves left behind; there are the gophers that burrow their way across the trails leaving mounds of uneven ground. And, don't forget the ground hog holes. These were also obstacles to the horses as well).

None of the above, are to be taken lightly to men and women walking, running, or jogging. Sounds like a fun place to jog, right?

Jogging in this pasture daily I learned that I must walk/jog/run with forgiveness.

Yes, forgiveness.

You see if I take each step running with my full weight dropping down onto the pasture and I hit one of those holes or uneven impressions... *CRACK.*

I have learned to walk/jog/run with a lighter landing and with much forgiveness in each step allowing my steps and my stride to glide across each hole or uneven ground with the ability to roll with it.

This, my friends, is how we are to walk this Earth: with forgiveness. Yes, we are to walk, not stand frozen afraid to move because of a foundation that is scary. We are to get out there and go. Walk, jog, run, and we are to do so with *forgiveness.*

CHALK TALK

Think about your life. Your trail. Your pasture that you are currently in.

How are you walking/running?
Are you landing hard on others?
On circumstances?
On excuses?
On feeling sorry for your current situation?

Landing hard can cause instant pain and serious injury to your soul, your spirit, or to others. Walking this earth without forgiveness can cause the strongest to stumble and fall or break.

Move forward, but do so with a smile, a light step and with forgiveness.

#39
The Wishing Will

A wishing *will* has a much better success rate than a wishing well. I don't think I would be going out on a limb too far to say that most people fit into one of these two categories:

Those that WISH
&
Those that WILL

Maybe you already know which one of these you fit into. Maybe you have noticed others around you that you can easily place into one of these categories. My hope is for those of you reading this that fall into the *wish* category... that you would be encouraged to shift over into the *will* category!

You see, all of us face things that are hard to do or no fun to do. Things we can see no good reason for doing, yet we find ourselves saddled with *having* to do it.

We all do things we don't want to do.

CHALK TALK

During those times we usually find ourselves 'wishing'. Wishing we were doing something else. Lot's of people wish to do many things. Wishing is very natural. But, why stop with just wishing?

Why not DO?

Why not turn your wish into a will?
Take your "That's something I *wish* to do someday" and turn into a "I *will* do that someday", and start right now!

Don't think you can't.
Don't think you're crazy.

Check these examples out:
Michael Jordan got cut from his high school basketball team!
A quote I love from Mr. Jordan;
"I've failed over and over again in my life. That's why I succeed."

Hank Aaron was 0 for 5 his first time at bat with the Milwaukee Braves yet went on to break Babe Ruth's Home Run Record.

Tom Landry, Chuck Noll, Bill Walsh, and Jimmy Johnson, all share the title of having the worst opening season records in the NFL. They all share the title of head coaches in the NFL that led their teams to 11 of the 19 Super Bowl victories from 1974 to 1993.

Albert Einstein did not talk until he was 4-years-old! He did not read until he was 7 years old! His teachers said he was mentally slow, unsociable, and adrift forever in foolish dreams. He was expelled from school. Albert somehow managed thereafter to contribute to explaining these small tiny things; light, time, energy and gravity. He explained that light energy came in chunks or quanta, now called *photons*. This explanation changed the way researchers thought about the nature of light. He discussed the Brownian motion that helped in proving the existence of molecules. He also gave forth explanation regarding the dynamics of individual moving bodies. And last, but not least, he explained the nature of space and time. I have no idea what any of the above means but I would think he didn't stop at wishing he could do something!

The bottom line is... don't quit!
Don't be defeated by your first, second or third go around.
Don't be the person that casts a wish into a bottomless WELL!
And then stand there and wish and wish and wish!
Be a person that casts your wishes into a WILL.

Turn your *I wish* into an *I will*.

#40
Encourage Courage

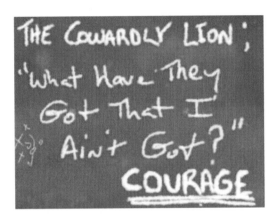

What is the craziest idea you have ever heard? Think about your friends; your bothers and sisters. Think about them sitting across from you BIG eyed and their faces lit up with fresh new excitement and great enthusiasm. Think about them not being able to get their words, thoughts, and ideas out fast enough.

Maybe they just realized what they want to be when they grow up. Maybe they have an idea that no one else has ever thought about. Maybe they have a vision of how something that exists could be better if.... Maybe they have an idea of a different way of doing something that goes totally against conventional wisdom.

How do you react? Have you given any of theses responses?
"*You can't do that!*"
"*That's not the way it's done!*"
"*That's Stupid.*"
"*You're crazy, people will laugh at you.*"
"*That will never work.*"

Have you ever heard any of these responses?
What if you tell that person..."*You can!*"
What if you tell a person..."*Go for it!*"

What if you tell a person..."*That's Cool.*"
What if you tell a person..."*I bet people laughed at Noah.*"
What if you tell a person…"*Make it work*"! *That would be awesome!*"

What difference would that make to them, to you, to their friends, family, school, community, boss, and THE WORLD!
Not just their world; Your World.

Encourage!

What good does it do to tell anyone they 'can't'?
Why do we as people discourage others? To what purpose does it serve?

One of my favorite quotes, *"I never thought much of the courage of a lion tamer. Inside the cage he is at least safe from people."* - **George Bernard Shaw**

I laugh at the humor of a lion tamer being more safe with lions than people. As an athlete, this is what I love about the world of sports; A good Coach doesn't tell a player or his or her team, *"You can't!"*

That is why I think it's important for young people to participate in athletics. It's all about YOU CAN.

Encourage courage!

It takes courage to be different, confident, and positive.
It takes courage to take on the impossible, the never been done before.
It takes courage to hear, *"You can't do that"*, and then GO DO IT.
That fires me up!

Encourage Courage in your players, your teammates, and your children.
It's not hard.
Tell them they CAN.
Teach them Courage.

CHALK TALK

1 Chronicles 28:20 (NIV)

[20] David also said to Solomon his son, "Be strong and courageous, and do the work. Do not be afraid or discouraged, for the Lord, God, my God, is with you. He will not fail you or forsake you until all the work for the service of the temple of the Lord is finished.

#41
X's and O's and U

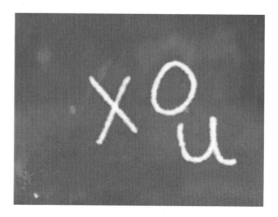

Coaches, draw up plays using X's and O's. There is great excitement during a timeout in a game when your coach is barking out orders and demonstrating his wishes. It's great to be on the bench, in the locker room, film room, or tape room as your coach demonstrates where you need to be and what you need to do. It gives you great confidence.

In other words, it's great to be an **X** or an **O**! When you are labeled an **X** or an **O** it means *you are in the game*!

What about when you are not practicing or playing? In *real* life it would be a shame for people to only know you for being an **X** or an **O**. Don't let the knowledge of you being an **X** or and **O** take away your **U**. Remember we *chalked* about this in Chalk Talk #6. You are **U** every minute of everyday. You are only an **X** and an **O** for a season.

U need coaching during timeouts.
U need to watch film, study tape.
U need to see **U** on the chalk board to know where to go and what to do.
A little coaching and direction on being **U** is necessary.

CHALK TALK

U are more than an **X** or an **O**.

#42
That's Not What We Do

Watching Alabama play Texas A&M a few years ago I saw Head Coach Nick Saban being interviewed before heading into the locker room at the end of the first half. The sideline reporter asked him about an unsportsman-like conduct penalty called against one of his players after scoring a touchdown. His response, *"That's not us. That's not our program. That's not what we do. We've never ever tolerated and we've never ever had it."*

Okay. Think about this.
People, this is great coaching.
Calling out a single player, a star player on National TV to say, "That's not *us*."

He didn't call out the player by his individual name. He said "*us*."
He didn't single him out.
He included the entire team.
"That's not *our* program."

He spoke of the single players infraction by including the entire team, and again when he said, "That's not what *we* do." When I see a leader lead this way it motivates me. He didn't have to say anymore than he said to convince me that what happened in the end zone after his player scored would never, ever happen again.

CHALK TALK

Coaches and parents, we can learn a lot from this. We must make very clear our expectations. We must speak them out loud and repeat them often. We must be consistent and steadfast in our commitment to accept nothing less than the bar we set.

Our children and our players are listening... *and* they are watching. Does anyone think Coach Nick Saban would ever act like the young man called for the penalty? No Way. I don't for one second think that anyone on his team thought behavior like that was acceptable.

But, we do make mistakes. All of us. Let those you coach or parent KNOW your expectations. Let them know by your words and your actions what you expect of them and from them.

They *will* rise to the bar you set.
They will from time to time fall short and a flag will fly... a penalty will be the consequence on the field... and perhaps extra running after the next practice.

Do not lower your bar! As a parent, and as a coach, *"THAT'S NOT WHAT WE DO."*

It's a beautiful thing.

#43
Face Masking

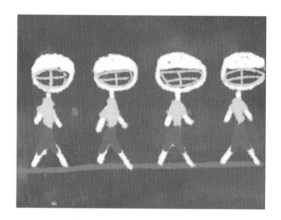

On one of my jogs around the football practice fields near my home I noticed as I ran by something odd about all of the kids. They were all almost identical in height and weight.

All have identical helmets.
All are wearing a practice jersey with no numbers.
All but two have the same colored pants, and only a few had different cleats.

This is a great picture that demonstrates the most important key to coaching: *knowing your players.* How do you tell who is who? Take away position and number and then ask yourself this question:

"What is the difference between my players"?

Let's consider the position first. You are a defensive lineman coach in football. You are coaching two defensive ends: a right defensive end and a left defensive end.

Do you coach both the same way?
Do you teach the right end to do certain things and tell the left end to do the same but opposite?

CHALK TALK

Let's consider the number. Numbers usually dictate a certain position or area a player plays.

Numbers 1-19 are usually a quarterback, running back, or Receiver.
Numbers 20 through 49 are usually running backs, defensive backs, line backers.
Numbers 50 through 79 are usually lineman.
Numbers 80 through 99 are usually tight ends and wide receivers.

Do you coach all of the numbers the same? The answer to both questions is obviously *No*. A coach must coach his team *individually*. He must coach behind the face mask's first.

It's tricky. Each one of these positions and players come with a different set of circumstances, emotions, reactions, and actions behind each *mask*.

The term *face mask* holds brilliant irony that we can all learn from. You can coach (or view) every person you meet in your life and not see beyond their *face mask*.

You can lump people into broad categories by assuming that their 'position' or their 'number' means they MUST be what the world says they are, judging them by either their position in life or number. But a good coach sees beyond the *face mask*.

We can learn from 'good coaches'. We too must see beyond the *face mask's* of others in order to *coach*. By coach I mean, a good friend, a brother or sister, father, mother, or teammate.

After all, deep down, don't you and I want others to see behind our *face mask* to see who we really are? So don't just look at a person's jersey number or their position in life and judge them accordingly.

See beyond their *face mask* to know who they really are.

#44
Boundaries

Boundaries. Have you ever watched the lines on a football field being laid out? It's a huge responsibility! Think of all the players, coaches, parents, and referee's that depend on those lines, that argue over those lines. The biggest and worst moments happen within those lines, AND outside those lines. These lines better be 'plumb and right'!

As I watched this the other day I thought to myself how it's the same in life. How important are our lines or our boundaries?

Do you even have boundaries? And if you do, how do you line your field? You have to start somewhere. A corner. A place to call home. Home is where we all start and if we get our boundaries right, we are *squared away* for life and end up back home.

So, the starting place is important. We need a reference point to return to, so that when our boundaries are faded, skewed, or damaged by weather and storms, we can re-chalk our boundaries again.

So, where do you start?
Where and what is your corner?
Are your lines solid, straight, and true?

Lining your field is a huge responsibility.

Where do you go to get instructions on laying out your boundaries? Who is influencing your playing field? When I was in school our coach lined the football field. It's the same in life. We all need a coach to line our field.

Who's helping you draw your lines?
Who's in your corner?

Philippians 4:8 (NIV)
[8] *Finally, brothers and sisters, whatever is true, whatever is noble, whatever is right, whatever is pure, whatever is lovely, whatever is admirable—if anything is excellent or praiseworthy—think about such things.*

Think about lining your field of life within these boundaries.

#45
What are you Thinking?

How many times have you done something *not so smart* and heard these words, *"What were you thinking?"*

Notice it is a rhetorical question. The only answer we might offer might be, "I wasn't thinking." Really? Maybe? But, maybe we should take some time to consider the following:

Where do you get your ideas?
Where do you get your beliefs?
Where do you get your desires to do any and everything you do?

Remember Chalk Talk #1, *Two Wolves Within*? Please go back and read it. I would ask you after you read it to think about your influences. Think about what you are taking in with your eyes, and your ears. Think about what you are hearing and seeing in your day to day routine and your actions.

Think about your friends
Think about those that you allow yourself to be near.
In other words... *think about why you think what you think!*

#46
Character Line

When have we gone too far? Have you ever just loved to watch a certain athlete or an entertainer do their thing? A running back cut, slice, twist, and turn? Or a pass rusher bull rush and speed rush, or a basketball player that can shoot the three, take it strong and slam it home? How about an entertainer who's live show is packed full of great songs, band musicians, lights, jumbo screens, and wall to wall fun?

I know I have a long list of favorites. A long list of my heroes, and yes, "idol's". It's tough admitting to having idols. Nothing wrong with admiring people, nothing wrong with looking up to people. But how do we know when we take it too far?

Think about this:

When we become more focused on their gifts and less focused on their character, maybe that's a good place to draw a line? All of our gifts come from God, all of them. We should celebrate our gifts as well as celebrate the gifts of our brothers and sisters. But, we should also keep in mind that character is what makes a person with, or, more importantly, without their gifts.

So take note of a person's character. Let that be a bigger reason for admiration.

And by all means, let's all work on our own character.
And let that character shine with our gifts.

#47
Hey... I didn't say it!

Proverbs 12:1 (NIV)
Whoever loves discipline loves knowledge,
but he who hates correction is stupid.

Whoa. That verse isn't trying to make friends is it? Which is really a point within a point: when we seek knowledge through discipline, when we allow ourselves to be corrected, seeking things that are good, things that are just and right, we often set ourselves up to be made fun of.

No one loves being corrected. It's easier just to do your own thing. So when you do show good work ethic while denying the things that maybe others are doing, that we know are not in line with good character, you often become a target to be ridiculed. There are always those that might call you, *goodie two shoes*, or they might say: "*You think you are so much better than everybody else.*"

Proverbs is a book totally devoted to *Wisdom*.

Read it. At least read some of it. Turn to any page. Read. See if you agree. Should you receive criticism for adhering to discipline as a path to becoming better, keep going and remember what Proverbs says about those that oppose correction.

#48
Flex Your Heart Muscle

You can play hard and sometimes play harder, right? Coaches are often encouraging their players to 'play hard, or play harder'. Right on!

Athletes, musicians, writers, entertainers; I want to encourage everybody to continue to play, but think on this; *love, or love harder.*

Don't worry. You can still be tough. In fact it's tough to love.
(Have you have heard of Jesus and what he went through to love you?)

It's easy to sit around and do nothing. It's hard to practice, to work out, to discipline yourself in sports or in the entertainment world. So it is with love. It's easy to sit around and do nothing: never smile, never say a kind word, never open a door for someone, never care about anyone other than yourself.

It's hard to say "I'm sorry" or to take extra time to see if your buddy is okay, or to give time to someone you may not like or think is cool. Or, to take a moment to pray... REALLY pray.

Play hard or play harder.
Love hard or love harder.

BRYAN KENNEDY

Love is mighty.
Receive it.
Give it.
Be mighty!
Flex your heart muscle!

#49
Picking Teams... Picking Friends

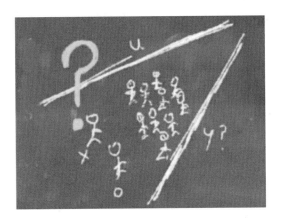

When we get a chance to play on the playground, in the gym, or park field, we go through the quick process of picking teams. This usually involves picking two captains, the flip of a coin to see who chooses their draft pick first, then each taking turns until all players are on a team.

Consider this:
How do the captains choose who to pick?
What if they don't know these potential players?
What if they are meeting or seeing them for the first time?
How do they choose?

Well, first, they certainly have to know what the game is and by what rules the game is to be played.

For example: if it is basketball, then naturally they might choose the tallest of the group. If it is football, they might choose who they perceive to be the quickest, the best passer, or the fastest, and so on.

Bottom line is this: the captains are making judgments based on what their goal is in building a team that they believe best will facilitate their chance of being successful and winning. They choose their teammates based on their perception of skills they think they might have, or by skills they know from experience they possess.

Well, what is the difference between picking teams and picking friends? Luckily you don't have to decide in an instant, but consider:

What is your goal in a friendship?
What do you know about the friend you are choosing?
Will this friend represent the 'team' you are building?
Will this friend be a loyal teammate through winning and losing?

Our parents may tell us we are judged by *the crowd we run with*, or more simply stated; *we are judged by our friends*.

You are the captain of your team of friends. You have a chance to pick your own team. We may not always get first pick. We may not always get top draft pick, but we do get to choose.

Think about your goals. Know your rules. Think about who you want on your team to accomplish your goals. And who will stay within your guidelines and rules in order for you to be a winner.

Choose wisely.

#50
Competition

The Merriam Webster Dictionary defines the word competition this way:

Competition

1. The act or process of competing; rivalry; the effort of two or more parties acting independently to secure the business of a third party by offering the most favorable terms
2. A contest between rivals; *also*: one's competitors

How do you compete with others? Let me ask you to consider something you might find different:

Concentrate on you!

The U.S. Army has that great slogan, "*Be All That You Can Be*". Those soldiers are preparing to fight wars! Real fighting! Not a Game. Are they focusing on their competition to ready themselves? NO. They prepare themselves to the max. They become all they can be, no matter what they may or may not face. What about Nike's brilliant ad campaign, "*Just Do It*"? Do what? Train, push, and ready.

Who?
YOU.

These are not targeted toward you thinking about your competition, or even considering your competition. Be all that YOU can be. Just do it... means YOU.

Every day YOU need to do all YOU can do!

Respect your competition no matter who or what it may be. But, don't waste your energy or spend time focusing on or worrying about your competition. Focus on YOU and what YOU can do every day to become your BEST.

Apply this to your life on and off the field and stage as well; outside the spot light that shines on you. Apply this to your daily life, your job, school, class, fraternity, sorority, family members, etc.

Be all you can be and just do it. Then no matter what, you are sure to be a winner.

#51
Get Coached

There's a big game coming up. You and your teammates wait in the meeting room for your coaches to come in. It's time to learn the game plan. The joking around ends and the smiles fade with the nervous awareness of the task ahead. Your coach approaches the chalkboard. But instead of marking on the chalkboard, he just gives a short speech, "Do whatever you want to do."

Is this the Coach you want in your life?

Is this really what you want? Is this not what we sometimes tell our parents, our teachers, our mentors? "I just want to do what I want to do." Well isn't it better when we're coached? Isn't it better when you allow yourself to be coached? A coach knows he or she cannot predict exactly what will happen, but they have the experience to coach you in the best way they know how, to achieve a successful result.

When your coach approaches that board they define your position with a clear X or O. They tell you without a doubt what it is you are to do and even give you back up plans for several scenarios, as they are well aware of the situation changing. It's good to know what you are doing.

It's good to seek out a coach that can help you identify the situation, and help you see your role, and how to come out in a winning place.

Bottom line:
Seek wisdom. Seek instruction. Seek discipline.

Get coached.

#52
Chalk Talk

My hope is that you seek out Chalk Talks. My hope is that you seek wisdom, seek those with experience, those you trust and those you know have got your back. Constantly seek those that have your best interest in their minds and hearts. Seek those that push you, challenge you and always seem to know what is best for you.

I realize sometimes your coach isn't near to give you a chalk talk to illustrate and show you exactly what your position or assignment is, or the possibilities and scenarios of what *might* happen next.

What do you do?

Try reading the book of Proverbs. Just pick it up and flip through it, you don't have to go *in order*.
I believe that book is loaded with; short, straight forward and to the point, Chalk Talks.

Remember there are two wolves within us all, which one are we feeding?

CHALK TALK

ABOUT THE AUTHOR

Bryan Kennedy is credited as a singer, songwriter, author, playwright, actor, keynote speaker and a Certified Professional Life Coach. Possibly best known for the three #1 Garth Brooks hits he penned, the Ole Miss football star has written numerous works. They include two plays, two animated cartoon scripts and two children books in addition to three books for adults. His own musical projects include; "Dis-Connected", "I'm so Jealous of Me", "Life.Love.Laugh" and "Made in the Shade".

An actor at heart, Kennedy landed a leading role in, "The Secret Handshake" starring Kevin Sorbo. Additionally, his play "Toe Roaster" is slated to become a motion picture. He will star in the acclaimed musical comedy's film adaptation.

Bryan's other literary works include;

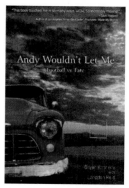

Andy Wouldn't Let Me

Charlie's Favorite Christmas

The Lost Dog (el perro perdido)

CHALK TALK

To purchase Bryan Kennedy's books visit;
Createspace.com
Amazon.com
bryanswebsite.com.

For Bryan's music visit;
http://www.cdbaby.com/Artist/BryanKennedy and
https://itunes.apple.com/us/artist/bryan-kennedy/id1390631.

To view videos of Kennedy's hits visit;
https://www.youtube.com/user/bryanswebsite?feature=watch.

Contact:
management@bryan-kennedy.com
Website: www.bryanswebsite.com

Social Media:
www.facebook.com/bryankennedyfanpage
www.twitter.com/UnderBryansHat
www.instagram.com/cowabungaboy

Made in the USA
Columbia, SC
28 April 2019